BLASTOFF! READERS, AN IMPRINT OF BELLWETHER MEDIA BY FLUTTERBEE

Blastoff! Readers are carefully developed by literacy experts to build reading stamina and move students toward fluency by combining standards-based content with developmentally appropriate text.

LEVELS

Level 1 provides the most support through repetition of high-frequency words, light text, predictable sentence patterns, and strong visual support.

Level 2 offers early readers a bit more challenge through varied sentences, increased text load, and text-supportive special features.

Level 3 advances early-fluent readers toward fluency through increased text load, less reliance on photos, advancing concepts, longer sentences, and more complex special features.

★ **Blastoff! Universe**

Reading Level

Grade
K

Grades
1–3

Grade
4

This edition first published in 2026 by Bellwether Media, Inc.

For information regarding permission, write to Bellwether Media, Inc., Attention: Permissions Department, 3500 American Blvd W, Suite 150, Bloomington, MN 55431.

Library of Congress Cataloging-in-Publication Data is available at www.loc.gov or upon request from the publisher.

ISBN: 9798893047943 (hardcover)
ISBN: 9798893048940 (ebook)

Editor: Kieran Downs   Designer: Brittany McIntosh

Printed in the United States of America, North Mankato, MN.

Table of Contents

What Are Hedgehogs?

Hedgehogs are small **mammals**. They have thousands of **spines** on their backs. There are many kinds of hedgehogs. They live in Africa, Asia, and Europe.

Western European Hedgehog Report

Some hedgehogs can weigh up to 3.3 pounds (1.5 kilograms).

They can grow to 12 inches (30 centimeters) long.

spines

Hedgehogs can be white, brown, or black. Their spines often have cream-colored tips.

Most have short fur on their bellies.

Most hedgehogs have pointed **snouts** and rounded ears.

They have short legs with big feet and large claws. They have short tails.

Spot a Hedgehog
rounded ears
spines
pointed snout

Sharp and Safe

Hedgehogs often live alone in forests and **grasslands**. Some live in **deserts**.

They often stay in **burrows** or under rocks. They also build nests.

Predators such as owls, hawks, and badgers hunt hedgehogs.

Hedgehogs curl into a ball
when danger is near.
Their spines keep them safe.

Hedgehogs often search for food at night. They eat frogs and **insects**.

They also hunt lizards and snakes. Hedgehogs sometimes eat bird eggs.

Growing Up

Female hedgehogs build a nest when it is time to have **hoglets**.

Most **litters** have four to six hoglets. Some can have up to 10 hoglets.

hoglets

Hoglets soon leave the nest with mom. They learn to search for food.

Hoglets leave mom when they are around four to seven weeks old. Time to hunt!

Life of a Hedgehog

Name of Babies

hoglets

Number of Babies

up to 10

Time Spent with Mom

around 4 to 7 weeks

Life Span

Glossary

burrows–tunnels or holes in the ground used as animals' homes

deserts–dry lands with few plants and little rainfall

grasslands–lands covered with grasses and other soft plants with few bushes or trees

hoglets–baby hedgehogs

insects–small animals with six legs and bodies divided into three parts

litters–groups of baby hedgehogs born at the same time

mammals–warm-blooded animals that have backbones and feed their young milk

predators–animals that hunt other animals for food

snouts–the noses and mouths of some animals

spines–sharp, pointed parts of some plants or animals

To Learn More

AT THE LIBRARY

Chang, Kirsten. *Baby Hedgehog or Baby Porcupine?* Minneapolis, Minn.: Bellwether Media, 2026.

Neuenfeldt, Elizabeth. *Forest Animals.* Minneapolis, Minn.: Bellwether Media, 2023.

Sabelko, Rebecca. *Grassland Animals.* Minneapolis, Minn.: Bellwether Media, 2023.

ON THE WEB

FACTSURFER

Factsurfer.com gives you a safe, fun way to find more information.

1. Go to www.factsurfer.com.
2. Enter "hedgehogs" into the search box and click 🔍.
3. Select your book cover to see a list of related content.

Index

The images in this book are reproduced through the courtesy of: Nynke van Holten, front cover (hedgehog), p. 21; LeManna, front cover (background), pp. 2-3; Laboko, p. 3; Serenity Images23, pp. 4, 6, 17 (hedgehog), 20; WildMedia, p. 7; NadyGinzburg, p. 8; Jussi Suvela, p. 9; Mirko Graul, p. 10; milanosss0/ 500px/ Getty Images, pp. 10-11; gihanart, p. 11; Les Stocker/ Alamy Stock Photo, p. 12; Erwan Balança/ Biosphoto/ SuperStock, p. 13; scigelova, p. 14; Kanyshev Andrey, p. 15; Brian Bevananthe/ Mary Evans Picture Library/ Pantheon/ SuperStock, pp. 16-17; Vaclav Matous, p. 17 (badgers); Zocchi Roberto, p. 17 (hawks); Albert Beukhof, p. 17 (owls); Ryzhkov Oleksandr, p. 17 (frogs); Nilanka Sampath, p. 17 (insects); Tomas Vynikal, p. 17 (lizards); Karl Van Ginderdeuren/ Buiten-be/ Minden Pictures/ SuperStock, p. 18; UQink, pp. 18-19; Tierfotoagentur/ Alamy Stock Photo, p. 21.